Big and Little

D0548620

written by Nina Filipek

illustrated by Louise Barrell

Filmset in Nelson Teaching Alphabet
by kind permission of
Thomas Nelson and Sons Ltd

The elephant is **big**.

HOW TO USE THIS BOOK

All children love to look at bright, colourful
pictures and indeed pictures play an important
part in the learning process.
By utilising colourful illustrations, this book
makes comparisons, and so in a fun way
develops the concept of opposites.
Work through the book explaining the opposite
nature of the objects shown and at the end of the
book see how many opposites your child can
identify.

Linda Coates, Cert Ed, MA

The mouse is **little**.

Big is the opposite of little.

The hippopotamus is **fat**.

The snake is **thin**.

Fat is the opposite of thin.

The car is **fast**.

The tractor is **slow**.

Fast is the opposite of slow.

A **sad** face.

A **happy** face.

Sad is the opposite of happy.

Cars go **over** the bridge.

Boats go **under** the bridge.

Over is the opposite of under.

The aeroplane goes **up**.

The parachute comes **down**.

Up is the opposite of down.

The kangaroo is **first**.

The penguin is **last**.

First is the opposite of last.

A **tall** man.

A **short** man.

Tall is the opposite of short.

The mountains are **high**.

The valley is **low**.

High is the opposite of low.

It is **light** outside.

It is **dark** outside.

Light is the opposite of dark.

A **cold** day.

A **hot** day.

Cold is the opposite of hot.

Look at this picture carefully.
Can you see any opposites?